Assemble Your Dream PC from Scratch

DIY Your Ultimate Computer Even If Technology is New to You

Aaron Lynas

Disclaimer

The information and instructions provided in this book are intended for general guidance and educational purposes only. The author and publisher make no representations or warranties regarding the accuracy or completeness of the content, and any actions taken based on the information in this book are done at the reader's own risk.

While every effort has been made to ensure the safety and effectiveness of the projects presented, the author and publisher are not liable for any injury, loss, or damage that may occur from the use of materials, tools, or techniques described in this book. Readers are encouraged to exercise caution and follow all relevant safety guidelines and manufacturer instructions when undertaking any of the projects.

By using the information provided, you acknowledge and accept these terms.

TABLE OF CONTENTS

INTRODUCTION

In a world increasingly driven by technology, there is something undeniably empowering about building your own personal computer. For many, the idea of assembling a PC from individual parts may seem like a task reserved for tech-savvy enthusiasts or IT professionals. But this book was written to challenge that myth — to show you that even if you're brand new to technology, you have what it takes to build a machine that meets your needs, reflects your style, and saves you money in the process.

This is not just a manual filled with technical jargon and overwhelming diagrams. Instead, it is a hands-on, beginner-friendly guide designed to demystify the PC-building process.

We'll start with the fundamentals — what a PC is, what each component does, and how to choose the right parts for your goals — and walk you through each step of the build, from unboxing your first component to hearing your machine power up for the first time.

Whether you're building a high-performance gaming rig, a reliable workstation, or a budget-friendly family computer, this book equips you with the knowledge, confidence, and practical skills to do it yourself.

Along the way, you'll gain a deeper understanding of how computers work, develop useful problem-solving abilities, and experience the satisfaction of bringing your custom machine to life with your own two hands.

Welcome to the world of DIY computing — a place where anyone can build something extraordinary from scratch. Let's get started.

CHAPTER ONE

Getting Started — Understanding the Basics of PC Building

1.1 What Is a Custom-Built PC and Why Build One?

A custom-built PC is exactly what it sounds like: a personal computer assembled from individually selected and sourced parts rather than bought as a pre-made system. Unlike mass-produced computers sold by big manufacturers, a custom-built PC reflects the specific preferences, goals, and budget of the person building it. It is not merely a machine; it is a project tailored to purpose — whether that be gaming, video editing, coding, office work, or simple everyday browsing.

But why go through the effort of building your own computer when there are so many ready-made options available? The answer lies in three key benefits: performance, customization, and value.

Performance is often the most cited reason people turn to custom builds. Manufacturers typically balance cost against performance, resulting in pre-built machines that cut corners on key components like graphics cards, RAM, or storage drives. By selecting each part yourself, you can ensure your PC includes high-quality components optimized for your needs.

For instance, a gamer may prioritize a powerful graphics card and a fast refresh rate monitor, while a video editor may need a multi-core CPU and large storage capacity. With a custom build, these needs can be specifically met — not approximated.

Customization is the second major reason. From the internal specifications to the case design and lighting options, building your own PC allows you to shape the look and feel of your system. Want a minimalist setup in a small form factor case? Prefer a transparent case with RGB lighting and liquid cooling? You're only limited by your imagination — and, perhaps, your budget.

Value is where many are surprised. Although it may seem like building your own PC would be expensive, it can actually save money in the long run. By avoiding unnecessary pre-installed software, brand markups, and bundled parts you may not need, you end up paying only for what you want.

Additionally, custom PCs are easier to upgrade. Instead of replacing an entire system when it's outdated, you can simply swap out components like your graphics card, RAM, or storage. Over time, this modularity translates to significant savings.

Ultimately, building your own PC is not just a means to an end; it's a learning experience that empowers you with deeper insight into how computers work. It's a gateway to self-reliance in a digitally dependent world.

Once you complete your first build, you may never look at a computer — or your own capabilities — the same way again.

1.2 Key Components of a Computer: A Beginner's Guide

Before diving into the assembly process, it's essential to understand what exactly makes up a computer. Each part has a specific function, and together they form a cohesive, functional system.

Think of it as constructing a house — you need a solid foundation, a supportive structure, efficient plumbing, and electricity. Similarly, a PC consists of several core components, each playing an indispensable role.

At the heart of every computer is the **Central Processing Unit (CPU)** — often referred to as the "brain" of the computer. The CPU performs all the calculations and logic operations necessary for programs and applications to function. It processes data, executes instructions, and governs the speed at which the computer completes tasks.

Brands like Intel and AMD are leading manufacturers, offering a wide range of CPUs designed for different workloads.

The **Motherboard** is the one that connects all other components. It's the main circuit board where the CPU, RAM, graphics card, storage devices, and power supply plug in. It also handles data communication between all the components. Choosing a compatible motherboard is crucial, as it determines what other parts you can use, such as the type of CPU socket or number of RAM slots.

Random Access Memory (RAM) serves as the short-term memory of your PC. It stores data that is actively being used or processed, allowing for quick access by the CPU. More RAM allows for smoother multitasking and faster performance in memory-intensive applications like video editing or gaming.

Next, we have the **Graphics Processing Unit (GPU)**, also known as the graphics card. While some CPUs have integrated graphics, a dedicated GPU is essential for gaming, 3D modeling, or video rendering. The GPU handles visual output to your monitor and significantly affects your system's ability to process graphic-heavy applications.

Storage devices come in two main types: **Hard Disk Drives (HDDs)** and **Solid-State Drives (SSDs)**. HDDs are cheaper and provide more storage capacity, while SSDs are faster, quieter, and more energy-efficient. Many modern PCs use SSDs for their operating system and main applications, while HDDs are reserved for larger file storage.

The **Power Supply Unit (PSU)** is often overlooked but is vital to system health. It distributes power to all components and must be powerful enough to support your system's needs. A high-quality PSU ensures stability and prevents damage to expensive components.

The Case, or chassis, houses all the internal parts. It comes in different sizes and styles, with airflow and cable management being key considerations. Some cases also include built-in cooling systems or space for liquid cooling.

Lastly, **cooling systems**—which include fans, heatsinks, and sometimes liquid coolers—are crucial to maintaining optimal operating temperatures. A well-cooled system ensures performance and longevity.

When assembled correctly, these components work together seamlessly, transforming a collection of parts into a powerful, personalized machine. Understanding what each part does is the first major step in demystifying PC building — and it's easier than you might think.

1.3 Busting Myths: You Don't Need to Be a Tech Genius

Perhaps the biggest barrier stopping people from building their own computer isn't money or time — it's fear. For years, a perception has persisted that building a PC is an activity reserved for engineers, IT specialists, or hardcore gamers. But the truth is quite different: you do not need to be a "tech genius" to successfully build a PC from scratch.

One of the most common myths is that building a PC requires advanced knowledge of electronics or coding. In reality, building a computer is more like assembling a LEGO set than performing brain surgery. Modern PC components are designed with user-friendliness in mind. They use standardized sizes, color-coded connectors, and intuitive layouts. Most parts only fit one way, minimizing the risk of making catastrophic errors.

Another widespread fear is the idea that one wrong move can ruin everything. While it's true that components are delicate and should be handled with care, they're not as fragile as many believe.

If you take standard precautions—such as grounding yourself to prevent static discharge and handling parts gently—the risk of damage is minimal. Manufacturers understand that many of their customers are first-time builders and have built safeguards into their designs.

Many beginners also worry about compatibility: "What if my parts don't fit together?" While compatibility is an important aspect of PC building, it's one that can be easily managed with proper research.

Countless online tools, such as PCPartPicker.com, help users verify that all their components are compatible. These resources flag potential issues like voltage mismatches or size constraints, taking much of the guesswork out of the process.

Some also believe that building a PC is time-consuming and complicated. In truth, most builds can be completed in a few hours or less. With a well-organized workspace and a bit of patience, even someone who has never touched a computer's internals before can assemble a working machine in an afternoon. And unlike pre-built systems, which may take days to ship and arrive preloaded with unnecessary software, a custom PC is ready on your terms — with only what you choose to install.

Finally, there is the myth that it's "not worth the hassle." This is perhaps the most misleading of all. While there is a learning curve, the skills you gain from building your own PC extend far beyond the initial experience. You'll not only understand how your computer works, but you'll also be better equipped to troubleshoot problems, install upgrades, and make informed decisions about future purchases.

This sense of empowerment and independence is invaluable in a digital age where technology is an essential part of everyday life.

CHAPTER TWO
Planning Your Build — Budget, Purpose, and Performance

Before a single component is purchased, before a single screw is turned, the success of your custom PC build rests on careful planning. This chapter guides you through the essential early decisions that shape your entire building experience.

From defining what your machine will be used for to balancing budget with quality, and finally choosing between popular brands and components, this stage of preparation transforms a random collection of parts into a system with purpose. Just as an architect drafts blueprints before breaking ground, your PC journey must begin with a clear and thoughtful plan.

2.1 Defining the Purpose: Gaming, Workstation, or Everyday Use

The first and perhaps most important question you must answer is this: *What do you want your computer to do?* A system designed for gaming will differ greatly in cost and configuration from one built for casual web browsing or professional creative work. Defining the purpose of your PC early on not only streamlines decision-making but ensures that every dollar you spend supports your specific needs.

Gaming PCs, for example, demand high-performance components, particularly in the graphics and processing departments. If you're aiming to play the latest AAA titles at ultra settings, your build will likely require a powerful dedicated graphics card (GPU), a multi-core CPU, and a high-refresh-rate monitor.

Games also benefit from fast storage, often necessitating an SSD, and generous RAM for smoother performance. Additionally, gamers often care about aesthetics—cases with tempered glass panels, RGB lighting, and enhanced airflow are common in such setups.

On the other hand, a **workstation PC** built for tasks like 3D rendering, video editing, software development, or data analysis prioritizes processing power, multitasking capacity, and often larger storage.

These systems may require high-core-count CPUs, professional-grade GPUs (such as NVIDIA's Quadro or AMD's Radeon Pro series), and ample RAM—sometimes as much as 64GB or more depending on the workload. For creators working with large media files, multiple high-capacity SSDs and additional cooling solutions are often necessary.

Lastly, **everyday use PCs** focus on affordability, reliability, and efficiency. These builds are perfect for students, remote workers, or families who need a machine for web browsing, video streaming, document editing, or casual gaming.

While they don't require cutting-edge specs, they still benefit from quality parts. A quad-core CPU, integrated graphics, 8–16GB of RAM, and an SSD for faster boot times offer more than enough for daily tasks at a fraction of the price.

By defining your PC's purpose, you avoid overspending on features you don't need and ensure your machine delivers the performance you expect.

It also helps narrow down a seemingly endless list of component choices. Just as you wouldn't buy a sports car for grocery runs, you shouldn't pay for high-end features you'll never use.

2.2 Building Within Your Budget Without Sacrificing Quality

Once your purpose is defined, the next step is setting a realistic budget. Budgeting for a PC build doesn't mean settling for poor performance or low-quality parts. It means prioritizing wisely and spending where it matters most. The beauty of building your own system lies in its scalability—you can invest in what you need now and upgrade later as your needs evolve or funds become available.

Start by deciding on a total maximum spend. Whether you're working with $500 or $2,000, break that total into categories based on your purpose. For gaming, a substantial portion—often 40% or more—should go toward the GPU. For a workstation, the CPU and RAM may take precedence. For casual use, a balanced budget across CPU, RAM, and storage will deliver the best value.

Avoid the temptation to splurge on high-end features that won't improve your experience. Ultra-fast RAM may sound impressive, but the performance difference for everyday tasks or gaming beyond a certain speed is often negligible.

Similarly, spending extra on a massive 1000W power supply when your build only needs 500W is inefficient and unnecessary. Spend strategically, and save room in your budget for essentials like a quality monitor, a reliable keyboard and mouse, and perhaps even an uninterruptible power supply (UPS) for protection.

Quality, however, should never be compromised. Cheap components often come with hidden costs in the form of instability, poor longevity, or incompatibility. This is particularly true for power supplies, motherboards, and storage drives.

A low-quality PSU, for example, can damage your entire system or fail prematurely. Always choose reputable brands with strong user reviews and solid warranties. Even budget builders can find reliable parts if they're willing to research and compare.

Another great strategy for stretching your budget is to **buy used or refurbished components**. While not advisable for every part—especially not for power supplies or hard drives—refurbished CPUs, cases, and even GPUs can offer excellent value when purchased from trustworthy sources. Just ensure they come with a warranty or return policy.

Additionally, **waiting for deals** can make a substantial difference. Sales events such as Black Friday, Cyber Monday, or seasonal promotions often slash prices significantly. Planning your build over a few weeks or months allows you to watch prices and strike when the timing is right.

Finally, remember that your first build doesn't have to be your last. Build what you can afford now, and plan for future upgrades. Components like the case, PSU, and even motherboard can often be reused in future builds or expanded with additional RAM or storage.

A budget-conscious approach focused on long-term value will serve you far better than one driven by impulse.

2.3 Choosing Between AMD vs Intel, NVIDIA vs AMD: What Really Matters

One of the most debated decisions in any PC build is choosing between competing hardware brands—chief among them, AMD vs Intel for CPUs, and NVIDIA vs AMD for GPUs.

Each company has its loyal followers, but when you strip away the fanfare, the right choice comes down to your specific needs and your budget.

AMD and Intel are the two giants in the CPU market, and each has its strengths. In recent years, AMD's Ryzen processors have garnered praise for offering excellent multi-core performance, making them particularly appealing for multitasking and content creation.

Ryzen chips typically offer more cores and threads for the price, which translates into better performance in applications like video editing, 3D rendering, and compiling code.

Intel, meanwhile, has traditionally held the edge in single-core performance, which matters for certain tasks—particularly gaming. Their recent Alder Lake and Raptor Lake processors also introduced a hybrid architecture combining performance and efficiency cores, pushing performance to new heights while maintaining power efficiency.

When choosing between AMD and Intel, consider how you'll use your machine. Gamers looking for peak frame rates might favor Intel's higher clock speeds, while streamers and creatives working with complex software may lean toward AMD's multi-threaded efficiency.

Additionally, pay attention to **platform features**—some motherboards offer better support for things like PCIe 5.0, DDR5 RAM, or integrated graphics, which can influence your decision.

NVIDIA and AMD dominate the GPU market, and both offer excellent options across a wide range of price points. NVIDIA cards are known for features like DLSS (Deep Learning Super Sampling), superior ray tracing capabilities, and broader support for creative software that leverages CUDA cores.

These features make NVIDIA cards particularly attractive to gamers seeking the best visual experience and professionals using apps like Adobe Premiere or Blender.

AMD, on the other hand, has made significant strides with its Radeon series, offering strong performance at competitive prices. Their latest GPUs compete closely with NVIDIA in raw performance while often consuming less power and coming in at a more accessible price point. AMD also offers features like FSR (FidelityFX Super Resolution), which competes with NVIDIA's DLSS and is compatible with a wider range of hardware.

The best GPU for your build depends largely on your resolution, the games or software you plan to use, and your monitor's refresh rate.

For example, someone gaming at 1080p doesn't need the most powerful card available, while a user with a 4K monitor or multi-display setup might benefit from a high-end GPU with more VRAM.

It's also important to evaluate **availability and price**. During periods of high demand, prices can fluctuate wildly, especially on graphics cards. Don't become fixated on one brand or model—if a competitor's card offers similar performance at a better price or with better availability, it may be the smarter buy.

In both CPU and GPU selection, your best strategy is to **focus on performance per dollar**, not brand loyalty. Use benchmarking sites and comparison tools to evaluate real-world performance in the tasks you care about. Look at temperature benchmarks and power consumption as well, especially if you're building in a compact case or have power constraints.

At the end of the day, AMD and Intel, NVIDIA and AMD—these are not battles to be won or lost. They're choices to be weighed carefully in the context of your goals, your software, and your budget. A well-informed decision is always better than a brand-driven one.

CHAPTER THREE

The Parts You'll Need — A Deep Dive into Components

Building your own PC is a rewarding experience, not only because of the cost savings or performance customization, but also because it offers an intimate understanding of the technology that powers your digital life. While the idea of selecting and assembling parts may initially appear daunting, breaking down each component's role and interconnection makes the process clearer.

3.1 The CPU and Motherboard: The Brain and Nervous System

If your PC were a human body, the Central Processing Unit (CPU) would be the brain. It performs all the logical, arithmetic, and control functions of the system—essentially directing the flow of information and ensuring that tasks are executed correctly and efficiently. Just like the brain governs the body, the CPU governs your computer.

Modern CPUs come from two major manufacturers: **Intel** and **AMD**. While both offer exceptional products, the choice between them often comes down to performance requirements, budget, and compatibility.

Intel chips are known for their high clock speeds and gaming performance, while AMD's Ryzen series shines in multitasking and productivity, thanks to more cores and threads at competitive price points. Selecting the right CPU depends heavily on your usage needs—whether you're gaming, creating content, or simply browsing the web.

Every CPU must be paired with a **compatible motherboard**, which functions like the nervous system—connecting and enabling communication between every component in your build.

Motherboards come in various **form factors** (ATX, Micro-ATX, Mini-ITX) and with a variety of chipsets that determine their features, such as support for overclocking, USB ports, and storage interfaces.

When choosing a motherboard, you must ensure it's compatible with your CPU—both in terms of **socket type** (e.g., LGA1700 for Intel, AM5 for AMD) and **chipset**. Beyond compatibility, consider what features you want. Do you need built-in Wi-Fi, Bluetooth, or multiple M.2 slots for high-speed storage? Do you plan to overclock your CPU, which requires robust power delivery systems and BIOS support? The answers will guide your selection.

A good rule of thumb: the motherboard should complement the CPU. It doesn't make sense to pair a high-end processor with a basic motherboard lacking essential features or durability.

At the same time, there's no need to overspend on a motherboard that offers features you won't use. Strike a balance based on your specific build goals.

3.2 Graphics Cards, RAM, and Storage: Power, Speed, and Capacity

Once the brain and nervous system are in place, your PC needs muscle and memory. This is where

Graphics Cards (GPUs), RAM, and **Storage** come into play. These components largely dictate how fast your system runs, how smooth your games or applications perform, and how much data you can store.

Graphics Cards (GPUs)

For gamers, creatives, and professionals working with intensive visual applications, the **GPU is arguably the most important component**. It handles rendering images, videos, and animations, and offloads visual processing from the CPU. A high-performance GPU enables you to play games at higher resolutions and frame rates, edit videos in 4K, and work with 3D modeling software seamlessly.

There are two major GPU manufacturers: **NVIDIA** and **AMD**. NVIDIA's GeForce series and AMD's Radeon series each offer a wide range of cards, from entry-level to enthusiast-grade. When selecting a GPU, consider your monitor resolution and refresh rate. A 1080p 60Hz monitor doesn't require a top-tier card, but a 1440p or 4K display, or a monitor with a

144Hz refresh rate, will benefit significantly from more powerful GPUs.

Don't overlook **VRAM** (Video RAM), the memory built into the graphics card. More VRAM allows the GPU to store larger textures and process data more efficiently, especially in modern games or creative software. For most 1080p gaming, 6–8GB is sufficient, while 4K gaming or professional workloads may require 10–16GB or more.

RAM (Random Access Memory)

RAM is your computer's short-term memory—it holds active data and instructions for programs that are currently in use. Unlike storage, which is persistent, RAM is volatile, meaning it clears when the PC shuts down. Having more RAM allows your system to handle more tasks simultaneously and reduces lag when switching between applications.

Today, **16GB of RAM** is considered the sweet spot for most users, including gamers and professionals. For basic usage like web browsing and office work,

8GB may suffice. Heavy multitaskers, content creators, or virtual machine users may benefit from **32GB or more**.

Equally important is **RAM speed** and **latency**. These metrics measure how quickly the memory can send and receive data. While faster RAM can marginally improve performance in certain applications—especially those reliant on memory bandwidth—it generally won't offer massive gains for everyday tasks or gaming beyond a certain threshold.

Ensuring your RAM is compatible with your motherboard and CPU is vital, as mismatched speeds or configurations can lead to performance issues or system instability.

Storage Drives

Your storage solution dictates how much data you can keep on your machine and how quickly your system boots, loads applications, and transfers files. Today, builders typically choose between two primary types: **HDDs (Hard Disk Drives)** and **SSDs (Solid State Drives)**.

SSDs are significantly faster, quieter, and more durable due to the absence of moving parts. The most common type is **SATA SSDs**, which offer solid performance at affordable prices. For even faster speeds, **NVMe SSDs** connect via PCIe lanes, providing up to six times the data transfer rate of SATA SSDs. These drives are ideal for booting the operating system, installing games, or editing large files.

HDDs, while slower, still have a place in budget-conscious builds or for mass storage. A 1–2TB HDD can be a cost-effective way to store large media files, backups, or programs that don't require fast load times.

For most users, a combination of a fast **SSD for performance-critical tasks** and a **larger HDD for storage** offers the best of both worlds.

3.3 Cases, Power Supplies, and Cooling Systems: The Unsung Heroes

Often overlooked by beginners, **cases, power supplies, and cooling systems** are vital to the functionality, safety, and longevity of your custom PC. While they may not directly affect framerates or processing speed, they ensure that every other component can operate at its best.

PC Cases

Your PC case serves as the chassis that holds all your components together. Beyond aesthetics, it plays a vital role in airflow, expandability, and even noise reduction. Cases come in various sizes—**Full Tower**, **Mid Tower**, and **Mini Tower**—each supporting different motherboard sizes and component configurations.

When selecting a case, consider how many **fans** it includes, whether it supports **radiators** for liquid cooling, and how much room it offers for **cable management**. Good airflow is essential; poorly ventilated cases can lead to overheating and performance throttling. Transparent side panels and RGB lighting may be appealing, but always prioritize airflow and build quality first.

Power Supply Units (PSUs)

The PSU is your PC's energy source, converting electricity from the wall into usable power for each component. Choosing a quality PSU is non-negotiable. A poorly made or underpowered PSU can cause instability, damage components, or even result in electrical fires.

Always opt for a **reputable brand** with **80 PLUS certification**, which ensures efficiency. The most common ratings are Bronze, Silver, Gold, and Platinum—the higher the rating, the more efficient the power usage.

For most mid-range systems, a **550W to 750W Gold-rated PSU** will suffice. If you plan on using high-end GPUs or overclocking your system, consider higher wattage.

Modular or semi-modular PSUs also help with **cable management**, allowing you to use only the cables you need, reducing clutter and improving airflow within your case.

Cooling Systems

Keeping your PC cool isn't just about comfort—it's about performance and longevity. As components work harder, especially during gaming or intensive workloads, they generate heat. Excessive heat can reduce performance and even damage components over time.

There are two main types of cooling: **air cooling** and **liquid cooling**.

Air coolers use heatsinks and fans to dissipate heat and are often sufficient for most users. High-quality air coolers are quiet, affordable, and effective—

especially when paired with a case that promotes airflow.

Liquid coolers, or **AIOs (All-In-One coolers)**, use a pump to circulate liquid through a radiator, which is then cooled by fans. While more expensive, they offer superior thermal performance and often look sleeker, especially in transparent cases.

Regardless of the method, good **case airflow** is crucial. Ideally, your case should have **intake fans at the front and exhaust fans at the rear or top**, creating a directional flow of air that cools components efficiently.

CHAPTER FOUR
Tools, Workspace, and Safety — Preparing for Assembly

Before a single screw is turned or component unboxed, the foundation of a successful PC build is preparation. Enthusiasts often emphasize choosing the right hardware, but the often-overlooked element that separates smooth builds from frustrating ones is how well a person prepares their tools, workspace, and safety protocols.

Much like a chef organizing their mise en place before cooking, a PC builder must carefully arrange their environment to ensure efficiency, comfort, and above all—safety for both themselves and the sensitive electronic components they'll be handling.

4.1 Essential Tools and Accessories Every Builder Needs

Contrary to popular belief, you don't need a full-blown toolbox to build a PC. In fact, many of the necessary tools are relatively basic and inexpensive. That said, having the right tools can dramatically improve your building experience, reduce errors, and prevent physical strain or damage to your parts.

At the very top of the list is a **Phillips-head screwdriver**, specifically a magnetic tip #2 screwdriver. This is your primary tool for installing virtually every screw in a computer—from securing the motherboard to mounting fans, drives, and the power supply.

A magnetic tip is particularly helpful, as it allows you to guide screws into tight spaces without the frustration of dropping them.

For those planning frequent builds or upgrades, a **precision screwdriver set** may be worthwhile. This set typically includes various sizes of screwdrivers, tweezers, and bits that are especially useful for handling small screws or working with delicate components like M.2 drives or graphics cards.

An **anti-static wrist strap** is also highly recommended. This simple device grounds you to prevent the discharge of static electricity that could damage your computer components. It clips onto an unpainted metal surface—usually the case—and helps dissipate any electrostatic buildup before it reaches the hardware.

Other helpful tools include:

- **Cable ties or Velcro straps**: Used to manage cables, improve airflow, and maintain a clean build.
- **Flashlight or headlamp**: Useful for illuminating dark areas inside the case, especially during installation of parts like the CPU power connector or case fans.
- **Thermal paste**: While most modern CPU coolers come with pre-applied paste, enthusiasts who plan to remount coolers or use aftermarket cooling systems often benefit from having a small tube of high-quality thermal paste on hand.

- **Plastic tray or magnetic parts dish**: Helps to keep screws and small components organized and prevents them from getting lost on the floor or rolling away.

Optional but useful accessories include an **anti-static mat**, a **compressed air canister** for cleaning components and dust, and a **hardware monitoring app** or USB drive with essential software tools for troubleshooting once the PC is up and running.

The goal is not to accumulate a massive collection of tools, but to be prepared with a few reliable, well-chosen items that make the assembly process smooth, safe, and enjoyable.

4.2 How to Create a Safe, Static-Free Building Environment

Your workspace is just as important as the components you'll be assembling. The right environment can prevent common mistakes, minimize stress, and protect your hardware from physical or electrostatic damage. Contrary to the image of messy, improvised builds on dining tables or carpeted floors, a proper building setup requires intentional design.

First and foremost, select a **clean, flat, and sturdy surface**. A large desk or workbench made of wood or metal is ideal. Avoid using surfaces made of glass, which can generate static electricity, or soft surfaces like beds, couches, or carpets, which are unstable and hazardous for both you and your components.

Clear the area of clutter. You'll need room to lay out your case, unpack and organize components, and keep your tools within easy reach. Many builders choose to place the PC case on the floor or a soft cloth next to the desk, then transfer it to the work surface once it's ready for internal installation.

Lighting is also a critical factor. Poor lighting increases the risk of misaligning parts or forcing connections incorrectly. Ideally, your space should be well-lit with adjustable lighting or direct overhead lights that reduce shadows. A desk lamp with a flexible neck can help illuminate tight corners inside the case.

Eliminate as many sources of static electricity as possible. Avoid working in rooms with wall-to-wall carpeting, especially during dry seasons when static buildup is more common. If you must work in a carpeted room, try standing on a rubber mat or using anti-static measures such as wrist straps and mats.

In terms of attire, avoid wearing wool, fleece, or synthetic materials that produce static charge. Opt instead for cotton clothing, and keep your sleeves rolled up.

Before handling any component, discharge yourself by touching a grounded metal object, such as the metal part of your computer case or an unpainted section of a radiator or metal desk frame.

Lastly, be mindful of **pets, food, and beverages**. While it might be tempting to snack while you work, crumbs and liquid are a death sentence for computer parts. The same goes for curious pets that shed fur or knock components off the table. Keep your workspace off-limits to distractions and contaminants.

Creating a dedicated, static-free, and well-organized workspace is an investment that pays off not just in the quality of your first build, but in your confidence and enjoyment of the process.

4.3 Understanding ESD and Safe Handling of Components

Perhaps the most underestimated hazard in building a PC is **electrostatic discharge (ESD)**. Invisible to the naked eye and often completely undetectable when it occurs, ESD is responsible for countless mysterious hardware failures—especially among novice builders unaware of its risks. Understanding how it works and how to prevent it is essential to protecting your investment.

ESD occurs when there is an imbalance of electrical charge between two objects, and that charge is suddenly transferred from one to another. You've likely experienced a mild form of this when touching a metal doorknob and receiving a slight shock. While that jolt is harmless to humans, a similar discharge can destroy the delicate circuits in a CPU, RAM stick, or motherboard.

The damage may not even be immediately apparent. ESD can weaken components gradually, leading to intermittent crashes, reduced performance, or sudden failure weeks or months after the build is complete. This makes ESD a "silent killer" in PC building, and one that is almost always preventable.

To avoid ESD, always wear an **anti-static wrist strap** and attach it to an unpainted metal part of the case. This grounds your body and equalizes the electrical charge between you and the component. If you don't have a wrist strap, make a habit of frequently touching the metal frame of the case before and during handling.

Handle components **by their edges**. Avoid touching the gold contact points or circuitry on RAM modules,

CPUs, or GPUs. Hold motherboards by their sides and never press down on the delicate pins or exposed surfaces. Even clean hands can transfer oils and moisture that degrade electronics over time.

When unboxing parts, place them on an **anti-static bag**, not directly on wood, cloth, or plastic surfaces. Contrary to popular belief, anti-static bags are designed to dissipate static—not insulate from it—so components should remain on or inside them until installation.

Also, never install components while your computer is plugged in. Even if the system is off, residual power in the power supply or motherboard capacitors can pose a risk. Make sure the system is unplugged from the wall and the power supply switch is in the "off" position.

It's also wise to build in a sequence that minimizes the amount of handling required. For example, installing the CPU and RAM on the motherboard before placing it in the case reduces the risk of bending pins or applying pressure awkwardly. Think through each step before acting, and never force a component that doesn't seem to fit—chances are, it's misaligned.

CHAPTER FIVE

Assembling the Core — Installing the CPU, RAM, and Motherboard

Assembling a computer can be an incredibly satisfying and empowering experience. Up to this point in your journey, you've acquired the necessary knowledge, gathered your tools, prepared your workspace, and selected your components with intention. Now it's time to build.

Among all the stages of PC assembly, perhaps none feel as significant as installing the "core" components: the CPU, RAM, and motherboard. These parts form the backbone of your computer, dictating its speed, responsiveness, and ability to multitask. While the task may appear daunting at first, careful handling, attention to detail, and a calm, methodical approach will turn what seems complex into a manageable and rewarding experience.

5.1 Step-by-Step CPU Installation and Thermal Paste Application

The CPU (Central Processing Unit) is often referred to as the "brain" of the computer, responsible for carrying out instructions and processing data. As one of the most delicate and expensive components in your build, its installation deserves the utmost care and precision.

Begin by unboxing your motherboard and placing it on a non-conductive surface—preferably the anti-static bag it came in. Locate the CPU socket, typically found near the center of the board and covered by a protective plastic cap.

On Intel motherboards, you will notice a metal lever that secures the socket cover. On AMD motherboards, particularly the AM4 or AM5 sockets, there's usually a locking arm that raises and lowers the socket mechanism.

Gently lift the lever or arm to open the socket. Now, retrieve your CPU and carefully remove it from its packaging by holding it at the edges—avoid touching the bottom where the contact pins or pads are located. These contacts are incredibly sensitive and even slight damage or contamination can impair functionality.

Align the CPU with the socket using the small triangle marker found on one corner of both the processor and the motherboard socket. This ensures the CPU is correctly oriented.

For Intel CPUs, gently lower it into the socket—do not force it. For AMD processors with pins, let the CPU drop into place under its own weight. Once aligned and seated, lower the locking mechanism to secure the processor.

Next comes the thermal paste. This compound helps transfer heat from the CPU to the cooler's base, facilitating efficient heat dissipation. If your cooler already comes with pre-applied thermal paste, you can skip this step. If not, apply a small pea-sized dot of thermal paste to the center of the CPU. Avoid spreading it manually, as mounting the cooler will naturally distribute the paste evenly.

Finally, install the CPU cooler. This process varies depending on the brand and model—some coolers require a backplate and mounting brackets, while others snap directly onto the socket. Follow the manufacturer's instructions closely, applying even pressure when fastening the cooler.

Be careful not to overtighten, as this could damage the motherboard. Once the cooler is secured, connect its power cable to the CPU fan header on the motherboard, usually labeled "CPU_FAN."

At this point, your CPU is seated, protected, and ready for action. You've taken the first critical step in building your dream PC.

5.2 Inserting RAM and M.2 Drives Without Damage

Random Access Memory (RAM) serves as the short-term memory of your PC, allowing it to access and manipulate data quickly. Installing RAM is a straightforward yet sensitive process that requires proper orientation and placement.

First, locate the RAM slots on the motherboard— usually two to four long, narrow slots near the CPU socket. Consult your motherboard manual to determine which slots to populate first for optimal performance. On most dual-channel boards, you'll insert modules into alternating slots (e.g., slots 2 and 4).

Before installing, press down on the locking tabs at the ends of each RAM slot. Then, hold the RAM module by its edges and align the notch in the gold contacts with the notch in the slot. Because the notch is slightly off-center, the module can only be inserted in one direction.

Gently insert the module into the slot and apply firm, even pressure until it clicks into place and the locking tabs snap back up. If done correctly, the RAM should sit flush with the motherboard and feel securely held.

Now, let's turn to M.2 drives—compact solid-state drives (SSDs) that connect directly to the motherboard, offering blazing-fast read and write speeds. Locate the M.2 slot, typically situated between the PCIe slots or near the CPU socket. You may need to remove a small heatsink or mounting screw before proceeding.

Hold the M.2 SSD at a 30-degree angle and insert it into the slot. Once inserted, gently press it down toward the motherboard and secure it using the mounting screw. If your board includes a heatsink, reinstall it to help manage thermals during heavy usage. Be cautious not to overtighten the screw, as the M.2 drive is thin and can crack under pressure.

These steps—installing RAM and M.2 storage— complete the essential memory and storage segment of your PC's core. They are easy to execute when approached with care and attention, and they make a significant impact on how quickly your system will operate.

5.3 Mounting the Motherboard and Managing Standoffs

Now that your CPU, cooler, RAM, and storage are installed, it's time to mount the entire motherboard into the PC case. This part of the process is exciting because it starts to bring your computer to life. However, it also presents the possibility of damaging components if not done correctly—especially when it comes to standoff alignment and grounding.

Begin by preparing your PC case. Remove both side panels and any pre-installed accessories that may obstruct access to the interior. Identify the rear I/O panel slot and install the I/O shield that came with your motherboard. This thin metal plate covers the motherboard's ports and helps protect against electromagnetic interference. Snap it into place from the inside of the case, ensuring it's flush and aligned.

Next, take a close look inside the case and locate the mounting holes for the motherboard. Cases are designed to accommodate different sizes (ATX,

Micro-ATX, Mini-ITX), so you'll need to match the holes in your motherboard with the corresponding standoffs in the case. **Standoffs** are small brass or metal pegs that elevate the motherboard off the case's surface. This is crucial because it prevents the motherboard's circuitry from shorting against the metal of the case.

If your case doesn't come with standoffs pre-installed, you'll need to screw them into the appropriate holes manually. Never skip this step or allow the motherboard to rest directly on the case. Count the number of mounting holes on your motherboard and install an equal number of standoffs in the corresponding locations inside the case.

Once your standoffs are correctly positioned, lower the motherboard into the case, aligning it with both the I/O shield and the standoffs. You may need to wiggle it slightly to ensure the ports fit into the shield and the holes line up with the standoffs. When everything is aligned, use the provided screws to secure the motherboard to the standoffs. Tighten the screws evenly in a crisscross pattern, but do not overtighten. The goal is to secure the board without bending or cracking it.

Finally, manage any cables that may be dangling inside the case. Tuck them away using cable ties or routing channels, keeping the interior clean and reducing the risk of interference during future component installations.

With your motherboard mounted and secured, the core of your PC is now complete. This milestone in your build marks a significant turning point—the heart of your system has been assembled with care, and you're now ready to move on to the next phase: connecting power, installing your GPU, and bringing your machine to life.

CHAPTER SIX

Completing the System — Graphics Card, Storage, and Power Supply

With your motherboard, CPU, RAM, and storage now in place, your PC is beginning to take shape. But to transform a lifeless chassis into a high-performance machine, three final components demand your attention: the graphics card, the storage drives, and the power supply. These parts are more than just accessories—they are critical to performance, reliability, and efficiency.

This chapter will guide you through the final stages of the hardware installation process, helping you install your GPU, manage your storage devices, and safely mount your power supply. When completed correctly, this phase not only maximizes system functionality but also ensures that your PC operates efficiently and safely under load.

6.1 Slotting in the GPU and Ensuring Compatibility

The graphics processing unit (GPU) is often the centerpiece of any performance-focused build, especially if your system is intended for gaming, 3D rendering, or video editing. Even for general-purpose use, a dedicated GPU can offload graphical tasks from the CPU, leading to a smoother user experience. As such, proper installation of this component is crucial to achieving your build's performance goals.

Begin by identifying your graphics card's dimensions and confirming that it fits within your PC case. Some high-performance cards are bulky and may occupy two or even three expansion slots in width, as well as a considerable length. Check the manufacturer's specifications to ensure compatibility with your case, especially if it includes front-mounted radiators or other obstructive components.

Locate the PCIe x16 slot on your motherboard, usually the topmost and longest slot. This is where the GPU will be inserted. Most motherboards support multiple PCIe slots, but using the top slot typically ensures maximum bandwidth and performance. If any case covers are obstructing the slot area on the back of your case, remove them with a screwdriver.

Carefully unbox your GPU and hold it by its edges, avoiding contact with any exposed circuitry. Align the card's gold connector with the PCIe slot and apply gentle, even pressure until the card clicks into place. The rear bracket of the GPU should line up flush with the case's expansion slot, and the card should feel secure in the slot without excessive force. Fasten the GPU to the case using the screws you removed earlier.

Next, connect the power cables. Most mid-to-high-end graphics cards require one or more PCIe power connectors—either 6-pin, 8-pin, or a combination. These connectors come from the power supply unit (PSU) and are typically labeled. Match the connectors to the GPU ports and plug them in firmly until they click. Ensure that the cables are not under tension or awkwardly bent, as this can stress the connectors over time.

With the GPU installed and powered, your system has now acquired its visual horsepower. The next steps involve adding and organizing storage and ensuring stable energy distribution throughout the entire setup.

6.2 SSDs, HDDs, and Cable Routing Made Simple

Storage is an often underestimated component, yet it plays a vital role in system performance, boot times, and responsiveness. Whether you're opting for a traditional hard disk drive (HDD), a solid-state drive (SSD), or a combination of both, proper installation and cable management can significantly affect your system's efficiency and aesthetics.

Modern builds commonly incorporate M.2 SSDs, which you may have already installed directly onto the motherboard. However, if you are using 2.5-inch

SATA SSDs or 3.5-inch HDDs, you'll need to mount them inside dedicated drive bays within your case. These bays are typically located in the lower front area or behind the motherboard tray.

Start by securing each drive in its respective mounting bracket or cage. Some cases feature tool-less designs that use clips or trays, while others require screws. Once your drives are mounted, locate the SATA data and power cables. The data cable connects each drive to the motherboard, usually at one of the right-angled SATA ports near the bottom right. The power cable, stemming from the PSU, typically has a flat, L-shaped connector.

Plug one end of the SATA data cable into the drive and the other into the motherboard. Then connect the power cable to the corresponding port on the drive. Repeat this process for each storage device you are installing. If you're using multiple drives, be mindful of airflow—avoid stacking them in a way that traps heat.

With all your drives in place, it's time to consider cable routing. This is where you can transform your build from cluttered to professional. Use the routing holes and tie-down points in your case to run cables behind the motherboard tray. This not only improves airflow but also makes future upgrades and troubleshooting significantly easier.

It's often helpful to route cables loosely at first, check that everything is connected properly, and only then secure them using zip ties or Velcro straps. Avoid pulling cables too tightly, and leave some slack for any future component repositioning.

By neatly organizing your storage drives and routing cables efficiently, you lay the groundwork for a tidy and reliable system that performs well and looks great.

6.3 Installing the Power Supply: Wattage, Connectors, and Safety Tips

The power supply unit (PSU) is the heart of your computer's electrical system, distributing power to every component and ensuring stable performance. Installing it correctly is critical not only for system operation but also for long-term safety and hardware longevity.

Before you begin, verify that your PSU has sufficient wattage for your build. A 500–650W PSU may be adequate for basic systems, but gaming or workstation setups with high-end GPUs often require 750W or more. Also consider the PSU's efficiency rating—look for models rated 80 Plus Bronze, Silver, Gold, or Platinum, which indicate better energy efficiency and less heat output.

Most modern PSUs are modular, semi-modular, or non-modular. Modular units allow you to attach only the cables you need, improving airflow and cable management. Semi-modular units have essential cables (like the motherboard and CPU power connectors) built-in, while non-modular PSUs have all cables permanently attached.

To install the PSU, first identify its mounting position in your case. Most cases place the PSU at the bottom, with a vent on the underside for airflow. If this is the case, ensure that the PSU fan is facing downward and that the vent is not blocked. Use the screws provided to secure the PSU to the rear of the case.

Next, begin connecting the necessary cables. These include:

- **24-pin ATX power connector**: This powers the motherboard and is the largest connector.
- **8-pin (or 4+4 pin) CPU power connector**: Usually located near the CPU socket on the motherboard.
- **PCIe connectors**: Power the GPU.
- **SATA power cables**: Power SSDs, HDDs, and other peripherals.
- **Peripheral connectors (Molex)**: For case fans or other legacy components.

When plugging in these cables, ensure they are fully seated and oriented correctly. Most connectors are keyed to fit only one way, so never force a connection. If a connector resists insertion, double-check its alignment.

Once connected, route the cables neatly through the case's management channels. This helps prevent airflow obstruction and reduces the risk of cables coming loose or rubbing against components. Bundle excess cable lengths and tuck them away using cable ties or behind the PSU shroud if your case has one.

One often overlooked but crucial step is to perform a final system-wide check before powering on. Make sure all power connectors are secure, components are seated properly, and there are no loose screws or wires that could cause a short circuit.

For safety, always plug your PSU into a surge protector rather than directly into a wall outlet. This protects your components from voltage spikes and extends the lifespan of your system.

With the power supply in place and everything properly connected, your PC is almost ready to come to life. This step marks the transition from hardware installation to system boot and configuration—a significant milestone in your journey as a PC builder.

CHAPTER SEVEN

Wiring It Right — Mastering Cable Management and Airflow

In the world of custom PC building, the visible hardware—such as the glowing graphics card or the stylish case fans—often steals the spotlight. However, beneath the surface of a clean and high-performing build lies a less glamorous but absolutely vital art: cable management.

Alongside it, effective airflow planning ensures your components remain cool and stable during intensive workloads. A well-organized interior not only pleases the eye but also maximizes thermal efficiency, minimizes electrical interference, and simplifies future upgrades.

This chapter dives into the foundational aspects of internal PC wiring and cooling. You'll begin by learning about the different types of cables and connectors you'll encounter. Then, you'll discover practical methods for arranging your cables in a clean, logical way. Finally, you'll explore how airflow works within a case and how strategic fan placement and cable routing can drastically improve system performance and longevity.

7.1 Understanding Cable Types: Power, Data, and Fan Connectors

Before you can master cable management, you must first understand the types of cables that inhabit your PC. These cables fall into three primary categories: power cables, data cables, and fan connectors. Each has a specific function and design and knowing how they operate is essential to building a system that is both tidy and functional.

Power Cables are responsible for delivering electricity from your power supply unit (PSU) to various components. The most prominent among them is the **24-pin ATX connector**, which powers the motherboard. You'll also use **4-pin or 8-pin**

CPU power connectors, typically found near the top-left corner of the motherboard.

PCIe power cables are necessary for most modern graphics cards and may come in 6-pin, 8-pin, or even 12-pin formats depending on the GPU model. Additionally, **SATA power connectors** supply electricity to storage drives and optical devices. In older builds, **Molex connectors** may also appear, powering fans or legacy accessories.

Data Cables facilitate the exchange of information between your components. Chief among these is the **SATA data cable**, a flat, L-shaped connector that links storage drives (like SSDs or HDDs) to the motherboard. **Front-panel I/O connectors** are another example.

These cables connect your case's power button, reset switch, and USB ports to corresponding headers on the motherboard. Modern builds also include **USB 3.0 or USB-C internal connectors**, which are often bulky and demand precise routing to avoid blocking airflow.

Fan Connectors are used to power and control cooling fans. Most motherboards have multiple **3-pin or 4-pin fan headers**, labeled as CHA_FAN or CPU_FAN. The 4-pin headers support pulse-width modulation (PWM), which allows the motherboard to regulate fan speed based on system temperature. In some cases, especially with RGB setups or custom loops, additional controller cables may be involved.

Understanding where these cables originate, where they need to go, and how they behave under stress or tension is the first step toward creating a well-managed build. By categorizing cables early in the process, you can begin to route them logically and with a clear end-goal in mind.

7.2 Clean Builds: How to Tidy Cables for Better Performance and Looks

The phrase "cable management" often conjures images of hidden wires and zip ties galore—and rightly so. Clean cable management not only creates a visually appealing system but also improves accessibility, reduces airflow obstruction, and prevents accidental disconnections. It's a form of craftsmanship that reflects patience, precision, and an understanding of your build's layout.

Begin by planning your cable routes before plugging anything in. Most modern PC cases include cutouts and grommets that allow you to pass cables behind the motherboard tray. This is your primary zone for concealing power cables, SATA lines, and fan wires. Lay the cables loosely at first, checking their lengths and endpoints. Do not tighten or zip-tie anything until you're confident about each connection.

Use the **case's routing holes** strategically. For example, the 24-pin ATX power cable can be routed through a cutout near the edge of the motherboard, allowing it to emerge cleanly next to its socket. CPU power cables often benefit from a hole near the top of the case. SATA and front panel connectors can route through lower cutouts to maintain a clean visual line.

Cable **length and flexibility** are crucial considerations. Overly long cables can create unsightly bulges, while stiff wires may resist bending and place stress on connectors. Modular PSUs give you an advantage here, letting you attach only the cables you need.

Use **Velcro straps**, **zip ties**, and **tie-down points** provided within your case to secure bundles and keep them from wandering into fan blades or heatsinks.

Pay special attention to the **visible areas**— particularly those that are seen through tempered glass side panels. Arrange cables into tight, parallel lines and avoid crossing wires at odd angles. Even a few seconds of care can transform a chaotic build into a sleek, showroom-worthy rig.

Equally important is managing the **rear side of the case**, where the bulk of unused cable slack will reside. Tuck excess lengths into drive bays, PSU shrouds, or behind removable panels. Although this area will likely be hidden from view, poor management here can still impact cooling and access.

Remember, cable management is not about perfection but about **intentional organization**. Strive for function first—ensuring nothing blocks airflow or becomes a hazard—then focus on form. In doing so, you not only enhance the lifespan of your components but also create a system that's easier to maintain, troubleshoot, and upgrade.

7.3 Airflow Optimization: Fan Orientation and Cable Routing

Airflow is the silent guardian of your PC's health. Without proper circulation, heat builds up inside your case, leading to thermal throttling, reduced performance, and, over time, hardware failure. Fortunately, airflow can be dramatically improved through thoughtful fan orientation and smart cable routing.

At its core, good airflow follows a simple principle: **cool air in, hot air out**. Typically, **intake fans** are mounted at the front or bottom of the case, drawing in cool air from the room. **Exhaust fans** are placed at the rear or top of the case to expel warm air. Most builds aim for a "positive pressure" setup—slightly more intake than exhaust—to prevent dust from being sucked into unfiltered openings.

The orientation of each fan determines the direction of airflow. Most fans have arrows etched onto the frame indicating airflow direction. When installing, make sure all fans cooperate, not conflict. For instance, a front fan should push air into the case, while a rear fan should push air out. Misaligned fans can create turbulent airflow and hotspots.

Once fans are properly positioned, cables must be routed to minimize obstruction. Even small clusters of cables dangling in front of a fan can reduce its efficiency. This is particularly true for GPU and front-panel cables, which often snake across the center of the case. Use the back of the motherboard tray to route as many cables as possible. When cables must cross open space, run them along the edges of the case, anchoring them securely.

Advanced builders may experiment with **custom fan curves** in BIOS or software, adjusting RPM levels to balance noise and cooling based on temperature thresholds. Others might invest in **fan hubs** or **controllers** to simplify wiring and control all fans from a single interface.

If your case supports liquid cooling or houses particularly hot components like high-wattage GPUs or overclocked CPUs, airflow becomes even more critical. In such scenarios, adding extra case fans or opting for higher CFM (cubic feet per minute) fans can make a significant difference. Just be mindful of the noise-to-performance ratio.

Air filters, commonly found at intake points, are also essential for long-term maintenance. They reduce dust buildup, which can insulate components and clog fans over time. Clean them regularly to maintain optimal airflow.

CHAPTER EIGHT
First Boot — BIOS, Troubleshooting, and System Tests

Congratulations on completing the assembly of your custom PC! After hours of careful planning, thoughtful execution, and meticulous attention to detail, you're now at the moment of truth: turning on your machine for the first time. But before you bask in the glory of your work, there are a few key steps to take to ensure everything runs smoothly and safely.

In this chapter, we'll guide you through the crucial steps you need to take when powering on your system for the first time. You'll learn how to access and navigate the BIOS (Basic Input/Output System), troubleshoot common issues if your PC doesn't power on, and safely stress test your system to confirm everything is working at peak performance.

8.1 Entering the BIOS: What to Check and Configure First

The BIOS, or UEFI (Unified Extensible Firmware Interface), is the first software your motherboard runs when you power on your PC. It's where your system conducts essential hardware checks before loading the operating system.

The BIOS is often referred to as the system's "first layer" of control, allowing you to configure key settings related to performance, security, and hardware functionality.

Accessing the BIOS

To enter the BIOS, press the designated key during the initial boot-up screen. Typically, this is either **Del**, **F2**, or **Esc**, but it varies depending on the motherboard manufacturer. You'll see a brief message on the screen during boot that tells you which key to press.

Once inside the BIOS, you'll be greeted with a series of menus and options. Here's what to focus on during your first boot:

Checking Hardware Detection

Before proceeding to configure anything, make sure the BIOS detects all your hardware correctly. This includes the CPU, RAM, storage devices, and GPU. Check the following:

- **CPU**: Verify that the correct CPU model is listed and that the motherboard recognizes it.
- **RAM**: Ensure the total RAM capacity matches what you've installed. If your motherboard has multiple DIMM slots, make sure each stick of RAM is recognized.
- **Storage Devices**: Look for your primary drive (SSD or HDD) and any additional drives you've installed. If you installed an M.2 drive, ensure it's detected properly as well.

- **Graphics Card**: If you installed a dedicated GPU, make sure the BIOS recognizes it, rather than defaulting to integrated graphics.

Adjusting Boot Priority

After confirming that your hardware is detected correctly, the next step is configuring the boot order. This setting tells the computer where to look first when starting up. Typically, you want your system to boot from a USB drive or DVD for OS installation, but after that, you'll want to prioritize your SSD or HDD as the main boot device.

To change the boot priority:

1. Go to the **Boot** tab in the BIOS.
2. Set the **Boot Device Priority** list to place your primary storage device at the top.
3. Save and exit the BIOS by pressing **F10** or following the on-screen prompts.

Enabling XMP for RAM

If you've installed high-performance memory, you may want to enable **XMP (Extreme Memory Profile)** in the BIOS. This allows your RAM to operate at its rated speed, which is usually higher than the default speed the system would otherwise use. You can find this option under the **Memory** or **Overclocking** section of the BIOS.

Adjusting Fan Profiles

Many motherboards come with fan control options within the BIOS. You can configure the fan speed curve to suit your cooling needs, ensuring the system stays cool during high-demand tasks.

Typically, a "Silent" or "Balanced" mode works well for general usage, but if you plan on heavy gaming or overclocking, you might opt for a "Performance" mode to keep temperatures in check.

Saving and Exiting the BIOS

After you've configured the settings to your liking, save your changes and exit the BIOS. Your system will reboot, and it's time to proceed with OS installation. However, if you encounter any issues at this point, don't panic—there are a few common troubleshooting steps we'll cover in the next section.

8.2 What to Do If Your PC Doesn't Turn On (Common Fixes)

It's the moment every builder dreads: you hit the power button, but nothing happens. Fortunately, before you begin to panic, remember that many startup issues are relatively simple to resolve. Here are some common problems and their fixes:

Power Supply Check

One of the first things to check is whether the power supply is properly connected and functioning. Follow these steps:

1. **Check the power switch** on the back of the PSU. Ensure it is set to the "On" position.
2. **Verify all power cables**: Double-check that the **24-pin ATX connector** is fully seated into the motherboard and that the **4/8-pin**

CPU connector is connected to the motherboard.

3. **Test the power supply**: If you have a PSU tester or spare PSU, test whether the power supply is outputting the correct voltages. If it's faulty, you'll need to replace it.

Loose or Unseated Cables

Sometimes, a loose cable or an unseated component can prevent the system from powering on. Ensure that all cables are securely connected to their respective components. This includes the power cables to the motherboard, GPU, and storage devices, as well as data cables such as SATA or PCIe connections.

Motherboard Power Button

If the motherboard power button is not working, check whether the **front panel connectors** (such as the power switch, reset switch, and LED cables) are properly connected to the motherboard. These connectors often require precise alignment, and if they're out of place, the system won't power on. Consult your motherboard manual for the exact pinout configuration.

Short Circuits or Standoffs

If your system is completely dead, it could be due to a short circuit caused by misplaced standoffs. Standoffs are small metal spacers that prevent the motherboard from making contact with the case. If a standoff is placed incorrectly and touches the motherboard, it can cause a short, preventing the system from powering up. Carefully inspect the standoffs and ensure they are correctly positioned under the motherboard holes.

Component Testing

If the PC still doesn't turn on, isolate potential problematic components:

1. **Remove non-essential components** (extra storage drives, additional RAM, etc.) and try to boot with just the CPU, one stick of RAM, and the power supply connected.

2. **Test the GPU**: If you're using a discrete graphics card, try connecting to the motherboard's integrated graphics (if available) to rule out GPU issues.

Error Codes and Beep Codes

Many motherboards display error codes or emit beep codes when there's a hardware issue. Refer to your motherboard's manual for details on interpreting these codes. They can often pinpoint the faulty component, such as RAM, GPU, or CPU.

8.3 Stress Testing and Monitoring Temperatures Safely

Once your system powers on and you're ready to install your operating system, it's time to make sure everything runs smoothly under load. Stress testing and monitoring your system's temperatures are crucial steps in ensuring your build can handle intense tasks like gaming, video editing, or rendering.

Why Stress Testing Is Important

Stress testing is the process of pushing your system to its limits to ensure that it can handle demanding workloads without crashing, throttling, or overheating. Stress testing is particularly important after building a PC, as it helps identify stability issues that may not be evident during normal usage.

Tools for Stress Testing

There are several software tools you can use to stress test your PC:

1. **Prime95**: A popular CPU stress testing tool that pushes your processor to its maximum capacity.
2. **FurMark**: A graphics card stress test that pushes your GPU to its limits, simulating intensive gaming or rendering loads.
3. **MemTest86**: A RAM stress test that checks your memory for errors.

4. **AIDA64**: A comprehensive benchmarking tool that tests various components, including CPU, RAM, GPU, and storage.

Monitoring Temperatures

While stress testing, it's essential to monitor your system's temperatures to ensure everything remains within safe operating limits. Modern CPUs and GPUs can handle high temperatures, but prolonged exposure to heat can lead to instability or damage.

To monitor temperatures, use tools like **HWMonitor**, **Core Temp**, or **NZXT CAM**. Aim to keep your CPU temperature under 85°C and your GPU temperature under 80°C during stress tests.

What to Do if Temperatures Are Too High

If your temperatures exceed safe limits during stress testing, there are a few things you can do:

1. **Check your cooling**: Ensure that your CPU cooler is properly seated and that all case fans are running as expected.

2. **Reevaluate your thermal paste**: If you suspect poor thermal contact, reapply thermal paste between the CPU and cooler.

3. **Improve airflow**: Consider adding additional case fans or adjusting the fan curves in the BIOS to increase airflow.

Running Tests Over Time

Don't just run a stress test for a few minutes—leave it running for several hours to truly push your system to its limits. Monitor your system for crashes, freezes, or any signs of instability. If your system passes prolonged stress tests without issue, you can be confident in its stability.

CHAPTER NINE
Installing the Operating System and Drivers

Now that your PC is assembled, the next crucial step in bringing your new system to life is installing the operating system (OS) and ensuring that all your hardware components are properly recognized and functioning. Whether you're installing **Windows**, **Linux**, or setting up a **dual-boot** system, the operating system is the bridge between your hardware and the applications you'll use.

In this chapter, we'll walk you through the entire process of installing an operating system, downloading and updating drivers, and selecting essential software to get you started. This will ensure your new PC is ready to handle everything from everyday tasks to high-performance applications.

9.1 How to Install Windows, Linux, or Dual-Boot Systems

Installing Windows

Windows is the most widely used operating system for gaming, general use, and professional applications. Installing Windows 10 or Windows 11 is a straightforward process that can be done via a USB drive or DVD. Here's how to get started:

Step 1: Prepare the Installation Media

1. **Download the Windows ISO**: Go to Microsoft's official website and download the **Windows 10** or **Windows 11** ISO file. Make sure to choose the correct version of Windows that matches your system's architecture (32-bit or 64-bit).

2. **Create a Bootable USB Drive**: Use the **Media Creation Tool** (Windows) to create a bootable USB. Simply insert a USB drive with at least 8GB of space, and the tool will

automatically download and install the OS onto the USB.

3. **Insert the USB Drive into the PC**: Once the bootable USB is created, insert it into the PC where you want to install Windows.

Step 2: Boot from the USB Drive

1. **Enter the BIOS/UEFI**: Power on the PC, and immediately press the key (usually **F2**, **DEL**, or **ESC**) to enter the BIOS.

2. **Set Boot Priority**: In the BIOS settings, go to the Boot menu and set the USB drive as the primary boot device. Save changes and exit the BIOS.

3. **Start Windows Installation**: The PC will boot from the USB, and you'll be presented with the Windows installation screen.

Step 3: Install Windows

1. **Choose Language and Region**: Select your preferred language, time zone, and keyboard layout.

2. **Install the OS**: Click on **Install Now** and enter your product key when prompted (if applicable). If you don't have a key yet, you can skip this step and activate Windows later.

3. **Partitioning the Hard Drive**: Choose the drive where you want to install Windows. If your drive is new, you may need to create a partition by selecting **New**. Windows will automatically create additional partitions for system files.

4. **Complete the Installation**: Windows will begin copying files and installing. This process will take some time, and your computer will restart multiple times.

Step 4: Initial Setup

Once the installation is complete, you will be prompted to set up your account, password, and preferences. Follow the on-screen instructions to complete the setup.

Installing Linux (Ubuntu as an Example)

Linux, particularly distributions like Ubuntu, is an excellent choice for users who prefer open-source software and customization. Here's how to install Ubuntu:

Step 1: Prepare the Installation Media

1. **Download the Linux ISO**: Visit the official **Ubuntu website** and download the ISO for the latest version of Ubuntu.
2. **Create a Bootable USB Drive**: Use a tool like **Rufus** (for Windows) or **Startup Disk Creator** (for Ubuntu) to create a bootable USB drive from the downloaded ISO.
3. **Insert the USB Drive into the PC**: Once the bootable USB is ready, insert it into the PC where you want to install Linux.

Step 2: Boot from the USB Drive

1. **Enter the BIOS/UEFI**: Reboot the system and press the appropriate key to enter the BIOS.

2. **Set Boot Priority**: Set the USB drive as the first boot device and save changes.

3. **Start Ubuntu Installation**: The PC will boot into the Ubuntu installer. Choose your preferred language and click **Install Ubuntu**.

Step 3: Install Ubuntu

1. **Partition the Drive**: Choose whether to install Ubuntu alongside your current OS (for dual-boot) or to erase the disk and use Ubuntu exclusively.

2. **Complete the Setup**: Select your time zone, keyboard layout, and user information. The installation will take several minutes to complete.

Step 4: First Boot

Once installation is complete, remove the USB drive and reboot the system. Ubuntu will load, and you can log in with the credentials you created.

Setting Up a Dual-Boot System

If you want to use both **Windows** and **Linux** on the same system, a dual-boot setup is the solution. During the installation process of Linux, you'll be given the option to install it alongside Windows. Linux will automatically partition the disk to make space for itself and create a boot menu to choose between the two operating systems at startup.

9.2 Downloading and Updating Drivers the Right Way

After installing your operating system, the next critical step is ensuring that your hardware components are properly recognized and functioning. This is done through the installation of **drivers**—software that allows the operating system to communicate with your hardware. Here's how to download and update drivers correctly:

Step 1: Installing Essential Drivers

1. **Graphics Card Drivers**: Visit the website of your GPU manufacturer, such as **NVIDIA** or **AMD**, and download the latest drivers.

Installing the latest graphics drivers ensures optimal performance for gaming, video editing, and graphic-intensive applications.

- o **For NVIDIA**: Download from the official **NVIDIA website**.
- o **For AMD**: Download from the **AMD support page**.

2. **Motherboard Drivers**: Go to your motherboard manufacturer's website (e.g., ASUS, MSI, Gigabyte), and download the drivers specific to your motherboard model. These include drivers for chipset, network, and audio components.

3. **Peripheral Drivers**: If you have peripherals like printers, webcams, or external devices, check their official websites for the latest drivers.

4. **Installing Drivers**: Once downloaded, run the installation files and follow the on-screen prompts. Many drivers will automatically install and configure your hardware.

Step 2: Updating Drivers

After installing the basic drivers, it's essential to keep them up to date. Manufacturers release updates to improve performance, fix bugs, and improve security.

1. **Using Device Manager (Windows)**:
   - Open **Device Manager** (type it in the search bar).
   - Right-click the device you want to update (e.g., graphics card, network adapter) and select **Update Driver**.
   - Choose **Search Automatically for Updated Driver Software**. Windows will search for the latest drivers and install them.

2. **Using a Driver Update Tool**: Tools like **Driver Booster** or **Driver Easy** can automate the process of checking for outdated drivers and updating them.

3. **Check for Manufacturer Updates**: Always visit the hardware manufacturer's website to check for the latest driver versions, especially

for important components like the GPU, CPU, and motherboard chipset.

Step 3: Driver Best Practices

- **Avoid Third-Party Sources**: While some third-party websites may offer drivers, always prioritize downloading drivers directly from the official websites to avoid malware or corrupted files.

- **Create System Restore Points**: Before updating critical drivers, especially GPU or motherboard drivers, create a system restore point. This allows you to revert your system to a previous state in case the update causes issues.

- **Monitor Performance**: After updating drivers, monitor system performance to ensure stability. Tools like **HWMonitor** can help you track temperatures, voltages, and clock speeds to make sure your hardware is functioning optimally.

9.3 Essential Software to Kickstart Your PC Experience

With your operating system and drivers in place, it's time to install the software that will make your PC a powerful tool for work, play, and everything in between. Here are some essential software categories and programs to consider:

1. Antivirus Software

Security is a priority, so install a reputable antivirus program to protect your system from malware, ransomware, and other threats. Popular options include:

- **Windows Defender** (built into Windows 10 and 11)
- **Avast**
- **Bitdefender**
- **Kaspersky**

2. Web Browsers

While most operating systems come with a default web browser, it's often worthwhile to install an alternative for better performance or features. Consider:

- **Google Chrome**: Known for speed and extensions.
- **Mozilla Firefox**: Privacy-focused and open-source.
- **Microsoft Edge**: Optimized for Windows with strong performance.

3. Productivity Tools

Whether you're working, studying, or managing personal tasks, you'll need software to help you stay organized and productive. Some essential productivity tools include:

- **Microsoft Office**: The gold standard for office applications (Word, Excel, PowerPoint).
- **LibreOffice**: A free alternative to Microsoft Office.

- **Trello** or **Asana**: For task and project management.

4. Media and Entertainment Software

For media consumption and content creation, consider installing the following:

- **VLC Media Player**: A versatile media player that supports virtually all file formats.
- **Adobe Photoshop** or **GIMP**: For photo editing and graphic design.
- **Spotify**: For music streaming.

5. System Optimization Tools

Keep your system running smoothly with software that helps optimize performance, clear junk files, and manage startup items:

- **CCleaner**: For cleaning up unnecessary files.
- **Speccy**: To monitor your system's health and hardware specs.
- **Defraggler**: For optimizing disk performance (especially on HDDs).

6. Backup Solutions

Don't forget to install backup software to ensure your important files are secure. Consider:

- **Acronis True Image**: For full system backups.
- **Google Drive**, **Dropbox**, or **OneDrive**: For cloud-based file backups.

7. Gaming Software

If you're building your PC for gaming, here are some must-have gaming platforms and utilities:

- **Steam**: The largest platform for PC gaming.
- **Epic Games Store**: Another popular platform with free games and exclusive titles.
- **GeForce Experience** (for NVIDIA users): To optimize game settings and keep your GPU drivers updated.

CHAPTER TEN
Upgrades, Maintenance, and Personalization

Building your own custom PC is an incredibly rewarding experience. But just as with any piece of technology, it's essential to understand that the journey doesn't end once your system is up and running.

A great PC is a dynamic entity—constantly evolving and improving with time, and offering plenty of opportunities for upgrades, personalization, and ongoing maintenance. Whether you're looking to extend the life of your system, boost its performance, or make it more aesthetically pleasing, this chapter will guide you through these important aspects.

We'll cover how to upgrade your PC without starting from scratch, how to care for it with cleaning and long-term maintenance, and how to personalize your setup to reflect your unique style. By the end of this chapter, you'll have the tools and knowledge to keep your custom-built machine running smoothly and looking great for years to come.

10.1 How to Upgrade Your PC Without Starting from Scratch

The beauty of building a custom PC is that it's designed to be upgraded over time. Unlike pre-built systems, where upgrades can be more limited, your custom PC is flexible and adaptable. You can replace individual components to improve performance or add new features.

This section will guide you through common PC upgrades that can be made without the need to rebuild your entire system.

Upgrading the CPU

Your CPU is the brain of your computer, and upgrading it is one of the most effective ways to improve performance. However, upgrading your processor requires compatibility with your motherboard's socket type.

Before making an upgrade, you should verify that your motherboard supports the new CPU by checking the manufacturer's specifications. For example, if you're using an Intel i5 processor and want to upgrade to an Intel i7, ensure that the motherboard's socket is compatible.

In some cases, upgrading the CPU may also require a BIOS update, especially if you're moving to a newer generation of processors. Always check the motherboard manufacturer's website for the latest updates.

RAM Upgrades

Another common and relatively simple upgrade is increasing your system's RAM. This is especially useful for users who run memory-intensive applications, such as video editing software, 3D rendering programs, or high-performance games. Depending on your motherboard, you may be able to add more RAM without replacing the existing modules, as long as there are available slots.

When upgrading RAM, ensure that the new memory sticks are compatible with your existing modules in terms of speed and capacity. Many motherboards support dual-channel or quad-channel configurations, which can boost performance by enabling simultaneous data access across multiple sticks of RAM.

Graphics Card (GPU) Upgrades

For gamers and content creators, upgrading the GPU can yield significant performance improvements. Whether you're looking to play the latest AAA games at higher settings or speed up your video rendering times, upgrading to a more powerful GPU is often the most effective solution.

Before purchasing a new graphics card, check that it is compatible with your system. Ensure that the card will fit in your case (graphics cards come in various sizes), that your power supply can handle the additional wattage, and that your motherboard has the appropriate PCIe slots.

Storage Upgrades

Upgrading storage can significantly improve both the speed and capacity of your system. Moving from a traditional HDD (hard disk drive) to an SSD (solid-state drive) can reduce boot times, speed up file transfers, and make general system use feel snappier. If you already have an SSD but need more space, consider adding a secondary drive.

For a more substantial upgrade, consider switching to an **NVMe SSD**, which uses the PCIe interface instead of the SATA connection, offering faster read and write speeds. Ensure that your motherboard has an available NVMe slot and that the drive is compatible.

Power Supply (PSU) Upgrades

As you upgrade components, particularly the GPU or add additional storage drives, your power requirements may increase. It's important to monitor the power supply and upgrade it if necessary. A higher-wattage PSU ensures that your system remains stable during heavy usage. If you're adding a more powerful GPU or multiple storage devices, upgrading to a more robust power supply with higher efficiency ratings (like **80 PLUS Bronze** or **Gold**) is essential to maintaining system stability and reducing energy consumption.

10.2 Cleaning, Dusting, and Long-Term Care

Regular maintenance and care are essential to prolonging the life of your PC and ensuring that it operates at peak performance. The two main concerns that affect your computer over time are **dust accumulation** and **thermal management**.

Cleaning Your PC: The Importance of Dusting

Dust can accumulate inside your PC case, especially around cooling fans, vents, and heat sinks. This can block airflow, raise temperatures, and lead to overheating, which can shorten the lifespan of your components. Regular cleaning helps keep your system cool and efficient. Here's how to clean your PC properly:

1. **Turn Off and Unplug the PC**: Always turn off your system and unplug it from the power source before cleaning.

2. **Open the Case**: Most cases have side panels that can be removed with a screwdriver. Once the case is open, you can access the internal components.

3. **Use Compressed Air**: The best tool for cleaning your PC is a can of **compressed air**. Gently blow the air through the various components, especially around fans, the motherboard, and the GPU. Keep the can upright to prevent liquid from coming out.

4. **Clean Fans and Vents**: Dust tends to collect on fan blades and in vents, so be sure to clean these areas thoroughly. If the fan is particularly dirty, you can use a soft brush to remove stubborn dust.

5. **Wipe Down Surfaces**: After using compressed air, you can wipe down the case and other external components with a

microfiber cloth to remove any remaining dust.

Maintaining Optimal Temperature and Airflow

To keep your PC running at optimal temperatures, you need to ensure proper airflow inside the case. Overheating can cause components to throttle performance or even become damaged. Here are some tips:

1. **Monitor Temperatures**: Use software like **HWMonitor** or **Core Temp** to keep track of your CPU and GPU temperatures. Aim to keep these below 80°C under load.

2. **Reapply Thermal Paste**: Over time, thermal paste, which helps transfer heat from your CPU or GPU to the cooler, can dry out. If you're noticing higher temperatures or if you've recently removed a cooler, it's a good idea to clean off the old thermal paste and reapply a fresh layer.

3. **Upgrade Cooling Systems**: If you find that temperatures are still high after cleaning, you

may need to upgrade your cooling system. This could involve installing additional case fans, improving airflow direction, or opting for liquid cooling systems.

Routine Maintenance

1. **Check System for Errors**: Periodically run system checks and scans to ensure everything is functioning correctly. Tools like **Windows Memory Diagnostic** and **CHKDSK** can help identify issues with RAM or hard drives.
2. **Backup Your Data**: Regular backups are critical in case of hardware failure. Use external drives or cloud services like **Google Drive** or **Dropbox** to back up important files and system images.

10.3 RGB Lighting, Custom Cases, and Making It Yours

Personalizing your PC setup goes beyond its functionality—it's about making it your own. Customization, particularly in terms of aesthetic upgrades like **RGB lighting** and custom cases, allows you to reflect your personal style and make your PC a true centerpiece of your workspace or gaming setup.

RGB Lighting

RGB lighting has become a popular way to add color and style to your PC build. Whether you prefer a subtle ambient glow or an all-out rainbow display, RGB lighting can enhance the look of your PC and set the mood for your gaming or work environment.

1. **RGB Strips**: These flexible strips are easy to install inside your case and can be placed along the edges of the motherboard, behind fans, or around the perimeter of the case for ambient lighting. They're typically controlled by software or a physical remote that allows you to change colors and effects.

2. **RGB Fans**: Many fans come with built-in RGB lighting. These provide a combination of cooling and visual appeal, with customizable lighting that can sync with

other components. Some software, such as **Corsair iCUE** or **MSI Mystic Light**, allows you to synchronize lighting across multiple components.

3. **Customizable RGB Components**: If you're looking for even more customization, consider RGB RAM, motherboards, and GPUs. These components often come with their own lighting effects, allowing for a fully synchronized and personalized look.

Custom Cases

Your PC case is not just a protective shell for your components—it's also an opportunity for personalization. With countless options available, you can choose a case that reflects your aesthetic preferences, from sleek minimalist designs to bold, futuristic looks.

1. **Modular Cases**: Modular cases allow you to customize the internal layout of the PC, enabling better airflow or unique configurations of hardware. Some cases even

come with customizable panels that let you add glass or acrylic to showcase your internal components.

2. **Windowed and Transparent Cases**: If you want to show off your build, consider a case with a transparent side panel or even a full-glass side panel. This allows you to display your hardware, lighting, and custom cooling systems in all their glory.

3. **Themed Builds**: For those who love to stand out, themed builds allow you to personalize the external appearance of your case with custom paint jobs, decals, or 3D-printed components. There are also numerous third-party accessories available for modifying the look of your case, such as custom cable sleeves or decorative accents.

CONCLUSION

As you close the final chapter of this book, you now possess the knowledge, skills, and confidence to build a fully functional, personalized computer from the ground up. What was once a daunting tangle of wires, components, and terminology has become an accessible and exciting pathway to creativity, performance, and empowerment. You've not only learned how to assemble your dream PC step by step but also how to maintain it, upgrade it, and truly make it your own.

Building your own computer is more than a technical exercise—it is a statement of independence. It signifies a shift from being a passive consumer of technology to becoming its master and creator. Whether you built your PC for gaming, productivity, content creation, or simply to challenge yourself, you've joined a growing community of hands-on builders who believe in the power of customization and self-reliance.

But remember, this isn't the end. It's just the beginning. Your PC will evolve with you. As new technologies emerge, you'll be equipped to adapt and innovate. As your needs change, your system can change with them. Upgrades, modifications, and performance tuning are all part of the rewarding journey of ownership. With every tweak and enhancement, your machine becomes a reflection of your unique vision and goals.

More than just a collection of parts, your computer is now a masterpiece of your own design—something built with intention, care, and knowledge. Embrace the confidence you've gained, take pride in your accomplishment, and continue exploring what's possible. The tools are in your hands. The future is on your motherboard. And the journey doesn't stop here.

Welcome to the world of DIY computing. You've built more than just a PC—you've built a skill set that will last a lifetime.